THE CLIMBING BOY.

A COMIC DRAMA,

(WITH MUSIC.)

In Three Acts.

BY

RICHARD BRINSLEY PEAKE,

AUTHOR OF

" THE EVIL EYE ;" " MASTER'S RIVAL ;"
" BOTTLE IMP ;" " MIDDLE TEMPLE ;" " THE DUEL ;"
" JONATHAN IN ENGLAND ;" " BEFORE BREAKFAST ;"
" COMFORTABLE LODGINGS ;" " HAUNTED INN ;" " PRESUMPTION ;"
" WANTED A GOVERNESS ;" " AMATEURS AND ACTORS ;"
" HUNDRED POUND NOTE ;" " CHANCERY SUIT ;"
" SMUGGLER COUNT," &c. &c. &c.

FIRST PERFORMED BY THE

ENGLISH OPERA COMPANY

AT

THE ROYAL OLYMPIC THEATRE 1832.

" I'll creep up into the chimney."
MERRY WIVES OF WINDSOR.

THE MUSIC COMPOSED AND SELECTED BY MR. HAWES.

LONDON:

JOHN MILLER, HENRIETTA STREET,
COVENT GARDEN.

(Agent to the Dramatic Authors' Society.)

1834.

Printing Statement:

Due to the very old age and scarcity of this book,
many of the pages may be hard to read due to the
blurring of the original text, possible missing pages,
missing text, dark backgrounds and other issues
beyond our control.

Because this is such an important and rare work, we
believe it is best to reproduce this book regardless of
its original condition.

Thank you for your understanding.

TO

SAMUEL JAMES ARNOLD, Esq.

My dear Sir:

I have two reasons in dedicating this Drama to you: the first is, that I have endeavoured to introduce on the Stage (in the part of *Mr. Strawberry*) those TRAITS OF HUMANITY which, during a confidential friendship for a period of twenty years, I have ever had the pleasure to observe in your character.

Secondly, and I am reminded by my title, " THE CLIMBING BOY," that when *I* was a *boy*, you first kindly instructed me *to climb*.

I am,

My dear Sir,

Your's faithfully,

January, 1834.   R. B. PEAKE.

DRAMATIS PERSONÆ.

MEN.

Mr. Strawberry, M.P. .... MR. BARTLEY.

Sir Gilbert Thorncliffe, M.P. .... MR. PERKINS.

Jacob Buzzard (in the service of Mr. } MR. W. BENNET.
  Strawberry) .... }

The Climbing Boy.................. MISS HENDERSON.

Jack Ragg (a Non-descript) .... MR. JOHN REEVE.

Mordaunt .... MR. F. MATTHEWS

Courtroll (Steward to Sir Gilbert) .... MR. MINTON.

Slinker (a Poacher) .... MR. SALTER.

Dick (Son of Jacob and Rebecca) .... MISS MAHANY.

Chiffonier (an Upholsterer) .... MR. HEATH.

Police Inspector .... MR. SANDERS.

Policemen—Servants—Voters—Poachers.

WOMEN.

Miss Prudence Strawberry .... MRS. C. JONES.

Rebecca (Wife of Buzzard) .... MISS H. CAWSE.

Rosalie de Monneville (Daughter of } MISS SOMERVILLE.
  Sir Gilbert) .... }

Lucy .... MISS NOVELLO.

Jenny .... MISS MELBOURN.

The two Misses Starchblossom .... MISSES APPLETON
                                        AND GOWARD.

The Scene of the first Act is on the Estate of SIR GIL-BERT THORNCLIFFE in the Country.

The Scene of the second and third Acts, in London; and two Nights are supposed to intervene between the first and second Acts.

THE CLIMBING BOY.

———◆———

ACT I.—SCENE I.

A Parlour in the House of Mr. Strawberry. *Breakfast Table laid. An open Door in the centre, through which the Garden is seen.*

Several Voters with blue favours in their hats enter. c. d.

Voters.

Huzza! Huzza! Huzza!
Strawberry and liberty!
May " Liberty and Strawberry " ne'er sever,
Strawberry and liberty,
The old True Blue for ever.

Enter Miss Prudence Strawberry. l. h.

Miss Strawb. Hoity, toity, John—Jacob—what's the matter?
On the lawn I hear a monstrous clatter. (*Voters bow.*)
Say, fellows—to resistance will you urge us?

1st Voter.   Fellow! Ma'am, I am, an independent burgess,
As member, we yesterday, by votes returned your
brother.

Miss Strawb. Did you? then, I prythee, now return with one
another,

Voters.

Thank ye, ma'am, but willingly we'd drink his health in bumpers,
Because, dy'e see, 'twixt you and me, we brought him in with
plumpers.

B

Chorus of VOTERS.

Thus told our tale, a little ale would not be thrown away.

MISS STRAWB.

(*Aside.*) We have some ale, both sour and stale, that must be thrown away.

(*To* VOTERS.) Gentlemen be pleased to walk round to the butler's pantry,

And there at ease, with bread and cheese, you then our brewing can try.

VOTERS.

Huzza! Huzza! &c. &c.

(VOTERS *exeunt, bowing.*)   C. D.

MISS STRAWB. Burgesses, indeed! impertinence—pushing in here—

Enter STRAWBERRY.   L. H.

My dear brother, you have overslept yourself this morning.

STRAWB. Ah! sister Prudence! my head—my head.

MISS STRAWB. The election dinner at the " Greyhound" —the quantity of wine!

STRAWB. I am afraid it was the quality, as well as the quantity. I drank as much red ink yesterday as would rule all the records of the kingdom; but it was the speechifying about liberty and independence that flustered me more than the other stuff—'Ecod! I am in an extraordinary predicament: to be sure I have fortune and influence, but suddenly, and almost without my own consent, I am returned Member of Parliament for our borough, here! (*They sit to breakfast.*)

MISS STRAWB. Very complimentary to you.

STRAWB. Hang their compliment; why can't they let me be quiet? I wish I could provide a substitute, as they do in the militia.—I am undone: another cup of tea.

MISS STRAWB. That which is done, cannot be undone!

STRAWB. Dreadful!

Miss Strawb. What is the matter?

Strawb. Muffin!—What is the matter? how can you ask—you, who know I shall be fifty-nine years old next birth-day?—look at me—I have got to make a maiden-speech!

Miss Strawb. I am sure you need not trouble yourself, while you are aware there is a Speaker in the House paid to do all that.

Strawb. That says nothing.

Miss Strawb. How has it happened that you have been elected?

Strawb. I have been endeavouring to account for it—I possess hundreds of nephews, first cousins, and second cousins; the variously distributed offspring of brothers, sisters, brothers and sisters-in-law, uncles and aunts—by some accident all my relations have votes for the borough. As a matter of state policy (as I have been informed), but don't let it go any further—it was determined that the candidate of the opposite party should be thrown over the bridge.

Miss Strawb. And was he?—(alarmed)—poor gentleman! he'd catch his death of cold!

Strawb. Hush!—And it appeared that no other method could be devised for securing the proper number of votes, but making me a member of Parliament against my inclination.

Miss Strawb. Never mind, there is one comfort under the misfortune; we shall save a mint of money in postage, as you can frank letters for nothing.

Strawb. I would pay the postage of the whole town, sooner than have the privilege.

Miss Strawb. Oh! what extravagance!

STRAWB. Extravagance—you are ever calling me to account about extravagance—(another lump of sugar)—you know that when I feel an impulse of humanity, I am distressed until it is vented—now, you fritter your compassion into small details—your charity is crumbled.

MISS STRAWB. Crumbled?

STRAWB. Yes!—When it was resolved in this district, during the long frost, that the opulent should supply their indigent neighbours with coals, I, in the warmth of my heart, proposed that a quantity should be given to them.

MISS STRAW. *I* also said a quantity!

STRAWB. Yes; a *certain* quantity—half a skuttle-full at a time. Sister, if you had to dispense a thousand pounds, you would do it methodically, in sixpences.

MISS STRAW. I contend that by a wide distribution, the greater good is effected; but come, come, my most bountiful brother—as a member of Parliament you can aid the cause of humanity.

STRAWB. True—so I can—so I can.

MISS STRAWB. You are a subscriber to most of the charitable London establishments; I have a list in my bag of all the associations of which you are a life governor—first, there is the " Magdalen."

STRAWB. Ah! poor perverted creatures!

MISS STRAWB. (*Reading the list.*) " The Foundling."

STRAWB. Lost little beings!

MISS STRAWB. " Suppression of Climbing Boys."

STRAWB. Ah! (*abstracted.*)

MISS STRAWB. " The African Society"—(*Looks at him.*)—I declare you have a black on your nose.—(*Touches it with her handkerchief.*)

STRAWB. And what has a black on my nose to do with the African Society? (*Rising.*)

MISS STRAWB. Why, my dear brother, you are not attending to me,—you are lost in thought.

STRAWB. 'Ecod! I wish somebody would *find me* in thought!

MISS STRAWB. But whereabouts in London is our ready-furnished house taken?

STRAWB. Why, if I was to name the place, as it is thirty-five years since I have visited the metropolis, I could not describe the situation.

MISS STRAWB. I hope it is not near the Parliament house?

STRAWB. Why?

MISS STRAWB. So unwholesome in that lower part of Westminster. As a proof—You never read in a newspaper of a debate in the House, but several members are troubled with *a cough.*

STRAWB. Ah! maiden-speeches, I suppose; but to London we must go—are our truuks all packed?

MISS STRAWB. I will ring for Jacob, (*rings bell,*) he is our superintendent.

STRAWB. A careful, quiet, pious man—a perfect treasure of a servant; how am I indebted to my colleague, Sir Gilbert Thorncliffe, for recommending him. Only think, my dear, of having one's top-boots cleaned by a person who could write an extempore sermon.

Enter JACOB BUZZARD. L. H.

JACOB. Did you ring, sir?

STRAWB. Is every thing ready for our departure to town?

JACOB. Yes, sir.

STRAWB. The travelling chariot?

JACOB. Yes, sir; I ha' driven the chickens and swept the cobwebs out of it.

MISS STRAWB. Did you look at the linch-pins?

JACOB. Yes, madam, and greased 'em with my spetticals on, to see all were right.

STRAWB. We shall start to-morrow. You, Jacob, will set off this evening to prepare for our reception in the house which has been taken for us in London.

JACOB. Ah, sir, we be going to a mortal sinful place—I do hope we shall return with as clear consciences as those with which we leave the country. I shall take the liberty, with your kind permission, to stop an hour or two on the road to see my wife and my child.

MISS STRAWB. Jacob, it is a pity you are parted from them; but your wife is still in the service of Sir Gilbert Thorncliffe?

JACOB. She do keep one of the lodges of Sir Gilbert's park, three miles off.

STRAWB. But, Jacob, isn't it rather dangerous leaving your young and pretty wife alone so much—ahem!—I did not mean any thing, sister.

JACOB. (*Aside.*) Ah! you meant summut.

MISS STRAWB. Well, go, Jacob, here is a present for your little boy; don't let him spend it all at once—make the best of your way to town. (*Exit.*) L. H.

JACOB. Thank ye kindly, madam; why it is a silver-penny, I declare.

STRAWB. A silver penny—Whugh—ha! ha! ha! " don't let him spend it all at once!"—Here, my old moralist, there's a sovereign to buy your wife a new cap: there, begone, and take your own time to say good-bye to pretty little Rebecca. (*Exit.*) L. H.

JACOB. And if little Rebecca had not been pretty, this sovereign would not have been sent to her—I've seen your sly looks through the honeysuckle-window, my master. Ah! this be a terrible deceitful world, and a good many of us will astonish each other when we come to be found out. I do hope to be cunning enough to drive off the evil day— a fair face and a little sanctity are main good helps to a man in my situation. (*Exit* JACOB.) L. H.

SCENE II.

Drawing-room at SIR GILBERT THORNCLIFFE'S.

Enter SIR GILBERT, *followed by* COURTROLL. L. H.

SIR GILB. What letters have you?

COURT. One only of consequence, Sir—it is on the subject so painful to you—it is from your daughter. As you have declined correspondence, she entreats me to procure the bearer of this letter an interview with you.

SIR GILB. You know that the misconduct of my—... of that unworthy girl, has withered my heart.

COURT. All may not be so bad as you conjecture; let me beg of you, Sir Gilbert, to hear what this person may have to say.

SIR GILB. Admit him, Sir—(COURTROLL *goes off.*) Some agent of her needy paramour; perhaps to demand the base born pledge—the proof of her guilt—ha! I know not now where the boy is concealed—whether he be dead or alive.

(*Re-enter* COURTROLL, *introducing* MORDAUNT.—*Exit* COURTROLL.) L. H.

MORD. I presume I address Sir Gilbert Thorncliffe; the

introduction of an entire stranger needs apology. Sir Gilbert, you have a daughter.

SIR GILB. Spare yourself further trouble, Sir—I never hear her name.

MORD. If my recital cannot awaken slumbering affection, it may, at least, claim common justice: by a perverse fatality, you have been led to believe your daughter guilty; nay, sir, be calm. As I am in possession of facts and proofs to place her innocence beyond all doubt, I entreat a few minutes attention.

SIR GILB. May I inquire your name, sir?

MORD. Mordaunt—an Englishman by birth, but many years a stranger to my native land. My profession is that of a minister of the Roman Catholic church: to prove to you that I am intimately acquainted with the misfortunes which have alienated an only child from your affections, I will briefly detail that the gallant Count de Monneville, (a French nobleman of ancient family,) during a visit to this country, became enamoured of your daughter.

SIR GILB. Proceed, sir.

MORD. You were prejudiced against the foreigner.

SIR GILB. And did not the sequel warrant my prejudice? The villain De Monneville clandestinely carried her off; she resided with him in a state of open libertinism, disgracing a name that had never known dishonour.

MORD. De Monneville's conduct, though marked with imprudence, was not dishonourable—the same roof sheltered not the lovers until they were married.

SIR GILB. Married, say you?

MORD. Legally married.

SIR GILB. Why was that marriage concealed?

MORD. The Count de Monneville had been betrothed by

his parents to the heiress of a neighbouring estate. He loved her not—but the apprehension of giving anguish to his aged mother induced him to solicit the concurrence of your daughter to keep the marriage secret, until he had the opportunity of divulging it. The Count, to make peace with his family, and preparatory to the public introduction of his beautiful English bride, left her for a short period on his journey to the chateau of his father. On that fatal journey, the Count was deprived of life!

SIR GILB. How!—continue, sir.

MORD. A few stages from Aix-la-Chapelle, where the Count bade farewell to his beloved wife, he met and dined with the officers of a regiment of chasseurs. One captain, a fiery-tempered, indiscreet young man, who had seen De Monneville with his youthful bride, threw out insinuations too gross to be misunderstood, and in too public a manner not to be resented. De Monneville demanded retraction of the words, and an apology; which being uncomplied with, they went armed into an adjacent field; and your unhappy daughter's husband was left weltering in his blood.

SIR GILB. And how, sir, became you acquainted with this?

MORD. At the holy altar, I joined their hands in matrimony. At the grave of the gallant de Monneville, I read his funeral service!

SIR GILB. Why—why has this important communication been witheld until this time?

MORD. Your patience, Sir. For a difference on a point of doctrine, I incurred the resentment of the principal ecclesiastic of the diocese. I have suffered a rigorous monastic imprisonment for six years. A new order of affairs released me. Returning to my former home, I found your daughter's letters, entreating me to come forward and substantiate her innocence. It appeared that she had made a vain appeal to your compassion; and to crown her misery, on her arrival in London, her child, a lovely boy, was conveyed away from her.

SIR GILB. (*With emotion.*) I heard of that calamity, sir.

MORD. For four long years has your daughter been in dreadful anxiety as to his fate, and every effort to discover him has been ineffectual. She has quitted her house in London, which had been purchased and furnished by the agents of De Monneville, and letting it, lives now in retirement.

(SIR GILBERT *rings bell, enter a* Servant.) R. H.

SIR GILB. Prepare refreshments in the next room, and let some one hasten to Mr. Strawberry's—desire my late old servant, Jacob, to come over to me instantly. (*Exit* Servant)—(*To* MORDAUNT.) Sir, I go this evening to London—if you will accept a seat in my carriage, we can fully converse on this painful subject, and I will endeavour to do my unhappy daughter justice. Be pleased to step into this room. (MORDAUNT *bows, and exit.*) R. H.

SIR GILB. So!—All my harshness: all my venomous feeling towards my daughter (inflicted because I considered her guilty) now recoils upon myself. But the boy shall be restored—she shall again be made happy. (*A tap at the door.*) Who is there?

Enter JACOB BUZZARD L. H.

JACOB. What be Sir Gilbert's pleasure?

SIR GILB. Come hither, Jacob. Where is the boy that was entrusted to your care about four years ago?

JACOB. The—the boy—sir? (*Trembling.*)

SIR GILB. Whence this confusion?

JACOB. You have taken me suddenly by surprise, sir.

SIR GILB. How! Villain?

JACOB. You told me to convey the little boy from your sight—I obeyed you.

SIR GILB. Have you not received an annual stipend for his support?

JACOB. Ye—yes, Sir Gilbert—and I delivered the little fellow to the care of (I hope) an honest man, who dwells on the common.

SIR GILB. Oh! then the child is safe. He must be immediately sent for—I must see the boy this night—ay, .before I start for London.

JACOB. It is now so late—I fear it will be impossible, Sir Gilbert.

SIR GILB. I will excuse your absence to your present master, Mr. Strawberry; it is of import that the child should be found to-night. You need not bring him here—no—let me see—Is not the western lodge of the park occupied by your wife?

JACOB. Thanks to your bounty, Sir—yes, it be.

SIR GILB. Then convey the child to the lodge—it is in my road to London. (*Half apart, but overheard by* JACOB.) I should not recognize the boy again were I to meet him; but to be assured of his safety, my heart would regain its ease. You hear, Jacob?

JACOB. If it be possible, your honour shall be obeyed.

SIR GILB. There cannot be any difficulty. Remember, at ten o'clock I shall be at the lodge—let me find you there with the boy, and do not fail. (*Exit* SIR GILBERT.)

JACOB. Here's a quandary! What is to be done? One lie leads to many; I took Sir Gilbert at his word—" that he never would see the brat again;" as for the stipend, curse

the money, it burnt a hole in my pocket. Where's that
poaching scoundrel, Dan Slinker? I gave the boy to his
care, but I never thought it worth while to inquire what
had befallen him since. It will be a dark night—I shall
have a chance of meeting Slinker—perhaps in the home
preserve. What's o'clock? (*Looks at watch.*) It will be
worth a short run there, at any rate. La! deary me, it
requires a deal of trouble to keep up a respectable character.
(*Exit.*) L. H.

———

SCENE III.

Night.   A Coppice.

Enter a Poacher, *cautiously ; he listens, and beckons on
three others.* R. H. 2 E.

GLEE.——(Poetry Selected.)

Over heath and over field
    He must scramble who would find us,
In the copsewood close concealed,
    With a running brook behind us.
Here we list no village clocks—
Livelier sound the pheasant cocks,
Crowing—calling round about,
As if to point their roostings out.
But many a bird shall cease to crow
E'er we from the copsewood go.
Underneath the old elm-tree,
There we'll drink right merrily ;
Feasting in the grassy lane
Here this hour, then gone again.

(*Exeunt, excepting the* 1st Poacher.) L. H.

1st POACHER. No! by the marks I left, the keepers ar'nt
been here, and I twigged them over a bowl of hot punch at
the Thorncliffe Arms. (*Whistles.*) Dan! Slinker!

Enter DAN SLINKER. R. H. 2 E.

SLINK. Curse your bawling !—loud enough to bring Sir Gilbert from the manor-house. Here—while I try this copse—you carry these long-tails to Knapp's Bush—you'll find four short-tails in the dry ditch. (*Gives pheasants in a bag to* Poacher.) The London coach will be up in ten minutes; put the bag under the old ash-tree, the guard will know where to look for 'un. (*Exit* Poacher *with bag*. L. H.) I arn't tried this here presarve these three weeks. Dang it, sin the passing of the Game Act, we've got good customers with the Lunnun poulterers now; but what's a poor man to do? There be no use in starving while one can poach a little—better risk being shut in jail, where we be sure o' board and lodging, and to be well taken care of, than die by inches o' hunger. (*The moon appears*.) Ah, mother white-face! I didn't reckon on you to-night—it look'd cloudy. I should like to *take the shine* out of you—(*looking off*), and some one comes this way—can it be Sir Gilbert, or a new gamekeeper? None of the old 'uns will touch I—seeing as how I makes it worth their while to go to sleep, and let me work in quiet. (*Retires*.) R. H.

Enter JACOB. L. H.

JACOB. If I have any luck, somewhere hereabouts, Dan Slinker may be loitering; this is his time—I will try the signal (*whistles*). Poor Dan and I have been great dealers in our day.

Re-enter SLINKER. R. H.

SLINK A friend, by your whistle.

JACOB. It is I, Dan ! (*in an under tone*) I, Jacob Buzzard!

SLINK. *You* here? then by gosh you wants summut—or you'd see me skinned alive, before you'd walk out this time o' night.

c

JACOB. What a grumbler!

SLINK. Grumbler! why it is you, and such as you and your masters, that have made me what I am.

JACOB. Why, Dan, you've put me in good company—well here you are, *innocently* bagging the pheasants.

SLINK. And who, when the game was bagged and sold, and all the danger over, who *innocently* shared in the spoil? who but you—you sanctified old villain?—it was you first tempted me!

JACOB. Softly, Mr. Slinker.

SLINK. When you were Sir Gilbert's head keeper and farm bailiff, you lured me to this life—you knew well enough that the wages of a labourer could not support a wife and seven helpless chicks!—You knew that I had a stubborn spirit that would not let me stand praying and begging at the poor-house door—no, no, if all at home were crying or dying wi' hunger, I could hardly do that.

JACOB. Come, Dan, I did not intend to hurt you.

SLINK. Instead of giving me constant employ at a little better wages, which you could ha' done without injury to your master (for I *was* willing to work), you persuaded me to turn poacher—and then—rot you! you threatened to lay me in prison unless I paid you more than half the produce o' the game.

JACOB. Softly—gently, my good Slinker—this is ill-tempered. I—I have sought you to-night, to ask you a question.

SLINK. I knew he wanted summut, I said so—dang the old hypocrite turning up the whites of his eyes in the moonshine!—Well, what be it?

JACOB. Where is that little boy I placed under your protection four years ago?

SLINK. Ha! ha! ha! What do you call *placing under my protection?*—O! it's like you—you canting sinner!

JACOB. Did I not bring the boy to you?

SLINK. Sartainly.

JACOB. And where is he?

SLINK. How should I know by this time—four years ago! I'm sometimes glad to forget what has happened four days ago. The boy may be sent to Botany Bay for picking pockets—

JACOB. Bless my heart! Tell me, how did you dispose of him?

SLINK. He was *disposed* of—let that satisfy you.

JACOB. Disposed of!—and did not your compassion—

SLINK. Compassion! was it a time for me to compassionate a stranger's brat, when seven of my own flesh and blood were fighting and scratching for the pen'north o' bread I could throw among 'em?—Aye!—and when their poor mother, too, was fainting for the want of it? (*shudders*) I ha' seen starvation enough around me.

JACOB. But the boy—Slinker, I will reward you nobly, if you can lead me to him.

SLINK. Impossible—I drove the little fellow, in a higler's cart, to Lunnun—and there I *abandonated* him.

JACOB. Undone! (*Apart.*) How shall I face Sir Gilbert?

SLINK. (*Aside.*) I shan't let out the secret that I sold the boy to a chimney-sweep—or old wicked will ax me for his share of three sovereigns!

JACOB. And you will give me no further information?

SLINK. No—that is all you will get out o' me.

JACOB. Then look to yourself, Mr. Slinker—(*threatening*).

SLINK. What, you'll peach, will you? I say, old 'un, this here is the air-gun you bought for me to knock down the pheasants quietly (*produces it*). These thingummes have been known to kill a man before now. You had better be off—afore it goes off—(*points it*)—I an't particular what I shoot.

JACOB. Dear me, how odd, Mr. Slinker—bless my soul and body, Mr. Slinker—(SLINKER *aims, he exits hastily.*) L.H.

SLINK. Ha! ha! ha! I've frightened the devil's prime minister—now for the long-tails. (*Exit.*) R. H.

SCENE IV.

Interior of a Park Lodge ; door leading to an inner room.

REBECCA *discovered ironing linen. Clothes-horse before the fire.*

REB. Dear, deary me! Ah! mine is an odd life, sure enough. I'm a married 'oman, and yet, to all intents and purposes, I'm almost single—shut up in this solitary park lodge—all my business is to open an old gate, that goes with such a scrauk, like cutting the throats of ten ravens at once— my inconvenient husband, Mr. Jacob Buzzard (*puts the iron to her face*) quite cold!—he hasn't been nigh me for these last ten days—to be sure he lives in another service—I must have one rather warmer than that (*changes iron*). Oh, why did mother ever marry me to him?—Ah! I know, when I consented, I thought of the song of Old Robin Gray. (*Sings.*)

" My father argued fair; and my mother did na speak,
    But she look'd in my face till my heart was like to break;
    So I gaed him my hand, but my heart was i' the sea,
    And auld Robin Gray was a gudeman to me."

Ah! so I took old Jacob for his riches—I took him for bet-

ter and for worse—but I found him worse than I took him
for.—By Giminy, I shall wake Dick (*looks through a door*); no
my dear boy's as fast as a church, therefore I will be as si-
lent as a church-mouse. Jacob wants to send my poor Dick
out to work already in the fields, but I'll iron and double-
iron for every body, sooner than the boy shall have his
strength broken down by early labour—here's a deal to do—
I'm afraid I have got too many irons in the fire. (*Knock at
door.*)

REB. Who is there?—Who's there, I say?

JACOB. (*Without.*) Who is here, indeed?

REB. My husband! Oh, gracious!—(*Runs and opens the
door. JACOB enters.*)—Why, Jacob, Jacob, how pale you look?

JACOB. (*Apart.*) That dang'd air-gun goes off without a
report—but I don't think he has hit me.—(*Feeling his back.*)

REB. What is the matter?

JACOB. Eh—I don't know, Becky,—nothing.

REB. Jacob, I can tell better: don't your wife understand
your looks?—Have you had words with your master?

JACOB. If I have any words wi' he, they be always kind
ones. Bless you, old master Strawberry is one of the soft,
cabbaged-headed gentlemen—he trusts me through thick and
thin—I arn't afeard of he as I used to be of my last master,
Sir Gilbert.—(*Clock chimes.*)—A quarter to ten!—zookers!
what is to be done?—(*Sits down thoughtfully.*)

REB. And is this all the consolation you can bring to your
poor wife, after so many days absence? I tell you what,
Jacob, it's my opinion you want some supper, old gentleman. What do you think, now, of sitting down, nice and
comfortable, with a boiled rabbit smothered with onions?—
(*He shakes his head.*)—Or, if you shake your head at a boiled

rabbit, what would you say to a Welsh rabbit, if you saw one before you?

JACOB. Curse all rabbits!—my head be too full to think of putting any thing in my stomach.

REB. Ugh! you are as cross as two sticks. What is the matter?

JACOB. That boy!—that boy!

REB. That boy!—Oh, you are recollecting poor Dick, your only son.

JACOB. Dick!—eh—aye—ah!—how is Dicky?

REB. You cold-hearted flint! — (*Mimics.*) —" How is Dicky?"—the boy has gone to bed. Why, our Dick grows as nice and genteel-a-looking young codger as ever you see. —I mean him to be a clergyman.

JACOB. A clergyman! pooh! how is he to get *his living?* It wants——What's o'clock?

REB. Well! when you are settling what *it wants* to be a clergyman, you ask—(*Mimics.*)—" *What's o'clock.*" Why, it is ten minutes to ten—it is mortal late. Does your lord-ship mean to sleep here to-night?

JACOB. I am going to Lunnun to-night, Becky.

REB. La! Jacob, what extraordinary conduct—(*Goes up.*)

JACOB. (*Apart.*) Sir Gilbert will be here directly: I know him too well to disappoint or thwart him—he'd probe the affair to its depth—my character will be blown—I shall lose the employ of Mr. Strawberry, and end my days in jail.— A lucky thought comes uppermost—Rebecca!

REB. (*Coldly.*) Well, Mr. Buzzard!

JACOB. Has Sir Gilbert Thorncliffe ever seen our Dick?

REB. Not since he was short-coated, poor child.

JACOB. You are sure?

Reb. Certain. Why do you ask?

Jacob. I mean to show the boy to Sir Gilbert, who will call here to-night, on his road to town. Go, wake him up, and make the child look as tidy as you can.

Reb. For the matter of that, Dick is always tidy—see how I plait his frills. It's a shame to wake him, though—he has recited " *How doth the little busy bee,*" and gone off bang to sleep, two hours ago.

Jacob. Go, love, wake Dick up: perhaps Sir Gilbert's seeing him to-night may build his fortune: who knows?

Reb. Do you really think it will do him any good?

Jacob. You say Sir Gilbert has not seen the boy for years; who knows but he may take a fancy to him?

Reb. Well, it is never worth while throwing away a chance. Ah! Jacob Buzzard, thee hast got a scheming head—(*Goes into room.*) Come, Dick, boy, jump up—Dicky —Dick!

Jacob. Ay, if my scheming head sometimes gets me into scrapes, it gets me out again. I am in a hobble now—Yes, it is the only plan to save me. Sir Gilbert only wishes *to see* the boy to-night; it is several years since *he saw* the other. The lads had the same coloured hair; and Sir Gilbert barely looked at the little discarded child before he was sent away, and it is not probable that the poor wretch will ever turn up again.—(*Chimes, and clock strikes ten.*)—Sir Gilbert will be here directly. Shall I tell Rebecca? No: she will not agree to my plan—she is too honest, till I can palaver her over. Hark!—the carriage!—(*Noise of the carriage heard without.*)—I tremble—Psha! coward, brace up your old sinews; you have been in worse messes than this. —(*Takes a light, opens door of the Lodge.*)

Enter SIR GILBERT *and* MORDAUNT.

SIR GILB. Well, Jacob, have you succeeded?—have you executed my commission?

JACOB. I—I—ha' done my best, sir.

SIR GILB. I am impatient to behold my grandson—for as such I must now acknowledge him. (*To* JACOB.) Produce the boy.

JACOB. He is gone to bed, sir—but Mrs. Buzzard will fetch him up again....perhaps you would not like to have him roused up?

SIR GILB. (*Impatient.*) Instantly, Jacob, instantly!

JACOB. Oh, by all means, sir. Rebecca, love—here's Sir Gilbert wants to see—a—the little fellow.

Enter REBECCA, *leading* DICK, *neatly dressed ; she combs his hair down.*

REB. (*Curtsies.*) Make your best bow, sir.

SIR GILB. Good evening to you, mistress Rebecca,—he appears in perfect health. My little man, your hand. (*The boy hangs back.*)

REB. He be shamefaced afore gentlefolks, leading so lonesome a life——

JACOB. (*Apart to* SIR GILBERT.) On the common.

REB. But he is as nice a boy as ever drew the breath of heaven, tho' I say it—and if—

JACOB. (*Puts his hand on* REBECCA'S *mouth.*) Hush, Rebecca, (*aside*) if *you* talk you will spoil all.—If Sir Gilbert has a mind to take a fancy to him, let him take it in his own way.

SIR GILB. (*Laying his hand on* DICK'S *head.*) Poor child! I have injured thee, and thy mother——

REB. Sir? (*Aside*) What does he mean, I wonder?— (JACOB *takes her up the stage.*)

SIR GILB. (*To* MORDAUNT.) I do not trace my daughter's features in his blooming countenance—does he re-call his father, the unhappy De Monneville, to your recollection?

MORD. (*After a pause.*) No! no! the boy is well favoured, too.

SIR GILB. He must have been lamentably neglected!

REB. (*Quickly.*) That I am sure he has not, sir.

JACOB. Hush! (*Apart to* REBECCA, *and pinching her.*)

REB. Oh! how you pinch, Mr. Buzzard. I won't have my Dicky run down, (*To* SIR GILBERT.) Sir, if you please, the boy can read and write, ay, and work a little with his needle too—you smile, sir, but it's handy, you know, if a button comes off——

JACOB. Rebecca!

SIR GILB. Humph! am I to understand then that he owes his education to you, Rebecca?

REB. Every bit of it—(*rubbing her hands*)—every morsel of it.

SIR GILB. You have managed this well, Jacob—you certainly have obeyed my orders in keeping this child from my sight, but you have brought him up in health and comfort—you shall not go unrewarded. (REBECCA *stares.*)

JACOB. I told you, sir—the boy was entrusted to the care of honest persons. I hope *we be considered honest.*

SIR GILB. And your wife—she has been a second mother to him.

REB. *Second* mother! Who was his first mother then, I wonder?

SIR GILB. You shall know in due time, my good woman—I intend the boy to go to London with me to-night.

JACOB. }
REB. } To night, sir?

Sir Gilb. Yes—I cannot bear the suspense——he shall accompany me in the carriage to-night,—to-morrow, he shall be restored to his fond mother's arms.

Reb. Oh! be joyful, then *I* am going to Lunnun, too—

Sir Gilb. Why, as you have kindly attended to the wants of the boy for years, I have no objection to your following us to town. But for that child, I shall not part with him until I have placed him in the embrace of his natural protectress.

Reb. His natural protectress!——I know your honour will take care of him till I see him again.

Jacob. Hush—hush—get the boy's hat and little great coat. (*Aside*) Dick's fortune's made—go, quick, Rebecca.

Reb. Well! I declare——(Rebecca *enters the room with* Dick.) Come along, my little man.

Jacob. My wife has become fond o' the boy, sir—he! he! women are such soft creatures. La! deary me—

Sir Gilb. Mr. Mordaunt; I have to apologize for this delay, but it forms a part of your mission—how fervently will poor Rosalie bless you, for having been the restorer of her child!—Jacob; quick with the boy to the carriage. (*To* Mordaunt) Come, sir. (*Exeunt* Sir Gilbert *and* Mordaunt.)

Re-enter Rebecca *with* Dick.

FINALE.

Reb.   The moon is up, the night is mild;
　　　　Farewell, farewell, my dearest child.

Sir Gilbert's Servant, *at door.*

　　　　The carriage waits.

Reb.   Another kiss;
　　　　Take this, and this, and this, and this;
　　　　The moon is up, the night is mild—
　　　　Farewell, farewell, my dearest child.

(Servant *leads* DICK *out.*)

REB. So bright and clear the evening sky—
Good night, my boy ; good bye, good bye.

(*Whistle without.*)

JACOB. Those infernal poachers again, now I darn't say
my soul's my own.

(Poachers *enter.*)

Old fellow, old fellow,
We know you've some ale that is mellow ;
And as you love to drink the best,
We'll taste it 'ere you go to rest.

(JACOB *brings on jugs of beer, hands them to the* Poachers.)

POACH. The tyrant gone, our labour's done,
We'll drown melancholy in ale and be jolly.

(*The nightingale heard without.*)

REB. List, list, to the jug, jug, jug, jug, jug.

POACH. We take to the jug, jug, jug, jug, jug.
&c. &c. &c.

END OF ACT I.

ACT II.—SCENE I.

A handsome Bed Chamber, Bed Furniture white, Chimney and Fire-place, Chairs, Toilet with Glass. Portrait of a Lady.

MR. STRAWBERRY *discovered in a Cap and Flannel Morning Gown.*

STRAWB. Well, thank goodness, it's day-light and I'm up (*puts out lamp on hob.*) I have slept very little; but we all know what a strange bed is. In the country, the charming tranquillity of one's chamber—but here, in London, the rattling of the coaches—the tramp of the police—the concert of the cats, and the chiming of the church clocks disturb one's repose abominably. (*A tap at the door.*) L. H.

Enter JACOB, *with a jug.* L. H.

Oh! the hot water: how did you sleep, Jacob?

JACOB. Purely, thank you, sir; a man with a clear conscience generally rests well.

STRAWB. (*Rising*) I observe you always contrive to lug in your conscience; what is that scraping I have heard in the wall for the last half hour?

JACOB. It must be the sweeping of the chimney in the next room, sir.

STRAWB. Sweeping of the chimney; by machinery, I hope?

JACOB. No, sir, it's one of them there little black chaps.

STRAWB. How dare you, Jacob, who know my ideas on the subject, permit such an atrocious action as employing a climbing boy.

JACOB. Sir, it warn't I—I couldn't find it in my conscience to do it; it were the housekeeper; she forgot it yesterday.

STRAWB. Then I wish the housekeeper was poked up the flue for her inhumanity. Poor injured infancy! why adhere to a custom which is as barbarous as it is unnecessary ? You know I never have allowed it in the country.

JACOB. No, sir, we be humane in the country.

STRAWB. Ah ! aye.

JACOB. Blessed be humanity ! we do it there with a live goose, tie his legs together, shove him head foremost down the chimney ; he flaps his wings, and we lug him up and down with a rope.

STRAWB. What !

JACOB. If the chimney be very wide, we take two live geese.

STRAWB. I never knew of this, Sirrah ; though I have often wondered what made the poor geese so dirty. I thought I purchased machinery : what became of it ?

JACOB. I think the rats eat it.

STRAWB. Mark me, Jacob, I never will be accessory to the infliction of this horrible cruelty, oppression, and disease to poor helpless children. Put the water in the dressing closet. (JACOB *enters closet.* R. H.) I can't contain myself, when I think of the inhumanity—the degradation—the—(JACOB *crosses behind.*) Never let me hear again of such an occurrence, while you remain in my service. (*Exit.*) R. H.

JACOB. No, sir, no. I'll take care (*aside*) never to tell you any more. (*Exit.*) L. H.

(*A short piece of descriptive music, accompanied by the rattling of the shovel. The* BOY *cries without,* "Sweep ! Sweep !" *The music continues. The Boy descends from the chimney with a brush and scraper in his hand ; he shakes himself, and pulls his cap from over his face, looking round with wonder.*)

BOY. Oh, dear ! this is not the chimney I went up ! I have come down the wrong flue ; how they will thump me !

D

Bless my soul! it is a bed-room; what shall I do? I dare
not get up again, for I was almost suffocated in struggling
through the narrow brick-work. What, if I went to the
door yonder, and called out " Sweep !" (*crossing.*) No, they
would say I came here to steal something (*sobs.*) Oh, what
a miserable life I lead ! I, who recollect a kind nurse, and
a comfortable home, when I used to lie down on a bed (*looks
at the bed.*) What is the matter with me? the bed was so
very like that (*creeping towards the bed.*) I could almost
swear that I have slept in this room—ay, fifty times—and
in this bed (*draws the curtains, which he blacks with soot by
his touch.*) In this glass, too, I used to peep at myself (*goes
towards dressing table.*) I hav'n't seen my face in a glass
since I have been a filthy sweep (*looks at himself, and utters
a cry of horror.*) What a fright! (*sobs*) they used to call
me "pretty boy;" what would they say, if they saw me
now? (*Retreats from table, the toilet cloth discovered soiled.*)
Oh, la! Oh, dear! (*sits on a chair thoughtfully.*) I am thinking how my hard-hearted master will beat me on the head
with a shovel, for coming down the wrong flue. He will be
in a thundering passion. What is to be done? (*discovers
the dirt.*) Oh, mercy, here's a chair I have made! (*Attempts
with his brush, and then with his sleeve, to wipe the soot off;
makes it worse; tries to erase the black from the toilette cloth
and curtains.*) There, now, it is all over with me. I *shall*
catch it.—Perhaps I had best jump out of the window, and
put an end to my misery at once (*turns, and suddenly per-
ceives the portrait.*) Oh, goodness, how my heart beats!
Now I know—now I am sure—that picture! (*kneels down,
and sobs.*) Yes! oh where is she now? (*Hysterically.*) Look
at me! smile at me! remember me—mother! mother!
mother !

(MR. STRAWBERRY *opens the dressing closet-door, and appears with his neck bare, a cloth over his shoulders, his sleeves tucked up, and an open razor in his hand.*)

STRAWB. Heyday ! what the deuce is all this ?

(*The* BOY *jumps up, sees* STRAWBERRY *with the open razor, and alarmed, runs and folds himself in the white bed curtains, and peeps.*)

Come out, you unhappy black imp ! Come out, I say !

BOY. You will kill me ?

STRAWB. I kill you, poor boy ? I ? Alas ! what has the world come to that I should be suspected ? Do I look so terrible ? Oh ! I forgot. (*Closes the razor and puts it away.*) Come out, you little imp !

BOY. (*Creeps out, and falls on his knees.*) Oh, Sir, if you have any mercy in your heart, forgive me !

STRAWB. Forgive you, for what ?

BOY. For coming down the wrong flue.

STRAWB. Do not fancy that I will hurt you, poor wretch ! You are cold, I dare say, and hungry ?

BOY. I am, indeed. But master says, we are to be bold fellows, and never mind cold or hunger.

STRAWB. I can't overcome the humane impulse I feel. Here's an object upon whom I can bestow my proper charity ! Do you know, my little fellow, that I am a subscriber to the Association for alleviating the miseries of Climbing Boys ? Come here ; give me your hand—give me your hand, I say ! Tell me, how came you in your present situation ?

BOY. I came down the chimney.

STRAWB. I know that—I mean, did your father consent to your becoming a sweep ?

BOY. I never had a father.

STRAWB. Poor wretch !

Boy. I remember my mother ! I think I do.

Strawb. Well, and who was she ?

Boy. She was a lady.   But don't say I said it.

Strawb. Why not ?

Boy. Because master and the other sweeps knock me about so, if I ever mention it ; they sneer at me, kick me, and call me " Gentleman Billy."

Strawb. Gentleman Billy ! poor Gentleman Billy ! What say you to being relieved from your rags and soot ?

Boy. Oh, sir ! I would pray for you for ever and ever, and—

Strawb. And what, poor boy ?

Boy. I was going to say I would sweep all your chimneys for nothing.   I had a mother once who nursed me kindly : who—(*turns towards the picture*) Should she be living ! Sir ! might I be so bold as to ask—how I tremble !—if you know who that lady is ?

Strawb. An odd question.   No, I only came from the country to this ready furnished house last night.   Why·do you inquire ?

Boy. Sir ! I—I— He never will believe me (*aside.*) Oh ! good gentleman—that is the picture of my nurse, and, I think, my mother ; it is, it is, indeed.

Strawb. (*With emotion.*) Eh ! what ? And shall I perhaps be the means of restoring a lost being to his mother, too ? (*Rings bell violently.*) It must and shall be done without a moment's delay. (*Extravagantly excited*) I am in such a rage at the cruel degradation of these little black human specks, that I could in a paroxysm tear my shirt to pieces. Ugh !

Boy. (*Apart.*) He is going to send for master, and he'll break my back ! I'm off.

(*The* Boy *is hastily making his way up the chimney.* Strawberry *runs after him, and pulls him down again by the legs.*)

Strawb. Come down I say, you naughty boy! Can't you be quiet and let me do a kind action? No, the cruel treatment this poor child has received has blighted all his hopes of humanity! I must positively speak to him harshly to make him comprehend my meaning. (*In a threatening manner*) You little rascal! do you hear?—I intend to buy your time of your master, have your skin washed, give you some new clothes, send you to school—there, that has made an impression on him! and—(*looks at his hands*) confound it, he has made an impression on me!

Enter Jacob l. h.—*he starts.*

Jacob. The devil and Doctor Faustus!

Strawb. Well, Jacob, what are you staring at?

Jacob. Oh, this be the little chap they are making such a bother about in the next room: they have lost the little chimney-sweep they sent up; his master thought as how he had gone to sleep, so he has lighted a straw fire in the grate to bring him down again.

Strawb. Lighted a straw fire beneath the poor wretch to bring him down! this clenches the affair: Jacob, you are a person of pious sensibility?

Jacob. I be, sir.

Strawb. You can appreciate my feelings—I—I—ahem! I intend to patronize this unhappy soot-coloured natural production. Wait here till I have settled the point with the inhuman wretch to whom he is sold or apprenticed. Be kind to him, or, exemplary as you are, I will give you warning without a character.   (*Exit.*) l. h.

Jacob. Well, this be the queerest freak! But I know

my master's humour. (*To* BOY.) There, don't stand shiver-
ing there. Oh, I was to be kind to him. (*In an affected tone
of civility*) Will you have a glass of water?

BOY. No, sir.

JACOB. That there old gentleman is going to be a friend
to you.

BOY. I am glad of that, for I have but one friend in the
world.

JACOB. And what be his name?

BOY. Jack.

JACOB. Jack! Jack what?

BOY. I only know him by the name of Jack.

JACOB. Only do know him by the name of Jack, he! he!
Smoke Jack mayhap! Birds of a feather do flock together!
he! he! And where does Jack live?

BOY. He lives—he lives out of doors; but he has the
kindest heart—he's a big fat boy, and has saved me many a
larruping. (*Looks at* JACOB.) He is only laughing at me! I
wish the kind-hearted gentleman would return!

Enter STAWBERRY, (*elated.*) L. H.

STRAWB. It is all settled!—it is all settled! your sooty
indentures are to be given up. Mr. Scroggins, your master
in the art and mystery of sweeping chimneys, has swept his
bandy legs out of the house, bag and baggage.

BOY. And I am not to follow him and cry " sweep" any
more?

STRAWB. You shall never cry again. Jacob, d'ye hear?
take this little fellow to the housemaid; tell her to wash him
as white as a snowball—gallop to the ready-made clothes
warehouse, order them to send several small suits—do not
lose a moment.

JACOB. But breakfast be waiting, sir.

STRAWB. Hang breakfast, sir! Is breakfast to interfere

with a point of humanity? it must be done before breakfast. I'll astonish my prim sister. Go with my servant, my little fellow—not a word—quick! Run, Jacob, and instantly transform my blackbird into a robin-redbreast.—(*The* BOY *attempts to lay hold of* JACOB'S *hand; he hastily withdraws it, and exeunt.*) L. H.—What will my sister say? What will the generality of the world say? Reprobate my conduct in the same manner they did when I chose to let my old horses end their days in the orchard without work, in preference to selling them to the proprietor of a sand-cart; abuse me for my folly, as they did when I filled the bellies of all the little ragged boys and girls in the parish, with beef and pudding, on Christmas days. They were the pleasantest dinner parties I ever had in my life, for all that; and I wish I was down in the country again, settling the ox-cheek soup and blanket distribution business at the poor-house, instead of having to write, and afterwards to repeat, a cursed maiden speech in another house—Ugh!—(*A tap at the door.*)—Who is there?

MISS STRAW. (*Without.*) Brother, are you dressed? Can I come in?

STRAWB. Oh, yes, my dear.

Enter MISS STRAWBERRY. L. H.

MISS STRAWB. Well, how did you sleep? Pah! London smoke, and London filth—that which they call cleanliness here. How do you find yourself?

STRAWB. (*Abstracted.*) Poor fellow! rescued from dirt rags, and misery!

MISS STRAWB. What, wasn't your bed comfortable? I was so particular to direct, in our new abode, that it should be all nice for you. Do you hear me?

STRAWB. I have no fault to find with the bed; it was clean, comfortable, and all the furniture, too.—(*Abstractedly, passes his handkerchief several times across his face, which blacks it.*)—It annoys me that the poor little fellow should imagine that I could injure him. Is there, then, such inhumanity marked on my countenance? Look in my face, sister.

MISS STRAWB. I do: and it is uncommonly dirty. My dear brother, where is all this come from?

STRAWB. What is the matter?

MISS STRAWB. (*Putting on spectacles.*) In my born days I never saw you in such a pickle.

STRAWB. Pickle!

MISS STRAWB. And you tell me your bed was clean and comfortable—(*Going towards bed.*)—Mercy! only look at the curtains! And here's a dressing-table! What a filthy chair!—ruin to one's best poplin.

STRAWB. Shall I tell her yet of the Climbing Boy?— (*Aside.*) No.

MISS STRAWB. Go; wash your face.

STRAWB. Pickle indeed! Pickle!

(*Exit into dressing closet.*)

MISS STRAWB. I have heard a great deal of London smoke and dirt, but I had not an idea that it was half as bad as this.—(*She blows her ruffles and shakes her dress.*)—Pooh! tut, tut! My visit in this indescribably filthy place will not last long. This is beyond all the disagreeables one meets with in the country; though even there, as mistress of my brother's house, I have my little trials and troubles.

COMIC MEDLEY.

How sweet in the woodlands, with neat house and lawn,
Serene to awaken, and taste the fresh morn.

AIR—" *Away with this pouting and sadness.*"
You may talk of the calm of a village,
Of the quiet of country life,
But your peace is destroyed by small pillage,
Your solitude soured by strife.

I am mistress—but then there's a master—
I cannot do all that I wish ;
So I'll sum up first one day's disaster,
And you'll own it a kettle of fish.

AIR—" *Our Polly is a sad slut.*"

I ring my bell for Mary, my maid, Dame Huggins' daughter,
A tidy servant she would be, remembering what I taught her ;
But she has got no head to think—is such a stupid Mary,
Whatever orders I may give, she always acts contrary ;
For when I say I'm not at home, if troubled with the vapours,
She'll shew in smart-dressed company, with me, my hair in papers,
And there they sit, full puff, and sneer, for half an hour poking ;
I only ask it privately—now is not that provoking ?

(*Spoken.*) Then the next thing is :—

OLD AIR.

Why, oh dear, what can the matter be ?
Dear, dear, what can the matter be?
Oh dear, what can the matter be ?
    The thunder has soured the beer !
Twelve feet under ground is the place where I stock it ;
How the thunder could get in the cellar—I lock it,
And safe keep the key in my dimity pocket,—
    Then how could the thunder get there ?
            Then oh, dear ! dear ! &c. &c.

AIR—" *The Groves of Blarney.*"

Then in the kitchen
(With many a flitch in),
Our maids are stitching,
    Their duty there.

It grieves me though, when
The boys and ploughmen
Behave so so—then
    It makes me stare.

AIR—"*Dame Durden.*"

For John kissed Molly,
And Dick kissed Betty,
And Joe kissed Dolly,
And Jack kissed Katty
And Dorothy draggle-tail ;
It is enough to drive one mad this kissing should prevail.

(*Spoken.*) But it all amounts to this :—

There is no luck about the house
When my sharp eye's away ;
The proverb says—" The cat asleep,
The mice will always play."

There's no luck, &c. &c.

(*Exit* MISS STRAWBERRY.) L. H.

SCENE II.

A Chamber at MADAME DE MONNEVILLE'S.

Enter ROSALIE. R. H.

Ros. Could I but deck with flowers the sacred ground where thou sleep'st in peace, I should have the mournful felicity of knowing that the same roses would soon bloom over thy mother's grave, dearest boy ! Thou should'st have wept for me—I should not have had to mourn thy loss. I shall not long sorrow for my child.

SONG.—(*Poetry selected.*)

1.

Gone is my light of youth,
And fled my days of pleasure,
When all was hope and truth,
And trusting without measure.

Blindly I believed
  Words of fondness spoken;
Cruelly deceived,
  Peace for ever broken.
What can charm me more ?
  Life hath lost its sweetness;
Weary lags the hour—
  Time hath lost its fleetness.
        Gone is my light o youth, &c.

2.

As the buds of May,
  Were the joys I cherished;
Sweet but frail as they,
  Thus they passed and perished ;
And the few bright hours
  Wintry age can number,
Sickly senseless flowers
  Lingering through December.
        Gone is my light of youth, &c.

Enter Lucy. L. H.

Lucy. Oh, madam, your agent, Mr. Chiffonier, the upholsterer, was here yesterday, and he has let your house with the furniture to an elderly lady and gentleman from the country.

Ros. Ah! the calamity I experienced there would not permit me to rest under its roof.

Lucy. I have often been surprised, ma'am, that you should allow your portrait to hang up in that house.

Ros. I see the reason of your dislike to my picture, painted in happier days, becoming the remark of strangers. I give you the commission now, Lucy, to have it removed —beg Mr. Chiffonier to bring it to me immediately.

Lucy. Yes,—ma'am, the last time I saw your portrait, it was hanging over the chimney-piece of the apartment in which you slept before you quitted your house. (*A double knock. Exit* Lucy.)

Sir Gilb. (*Without.*) This way, is she?

Ros. Ah, my father's voice!

Enter Sir Gilbert Thorncliffe. l. h.

Sir Gilb. Rosalie! My daughter! (*Rosalie rushes to him, falls on her knees, and kisses his hands.*)

Ros. Father! beloved father! forgive your unhappy and repentant fugitive.

Sir Gilb. Rise, Rosalie; with this fond embrace all shall be forgotten—all pardoned.

Ros. Oh! this is the first gleam of bliss my heart has experienced for years! Pardoned!—yes, pardoned—and again in a father's embrace!

Sir Gilb. Calm yourself, Rosalie—I have not a shade of displeasure nor of grief left; I behold your transport at again being reconciled to a parent. What, if I could add to it by divulging a secret?

Ros. I pray, sir, not at this moment—my heart is too full.

Sir Gilb. You had a son—

Ros. (*Suddenly starting up.*) What say you?—Does he live?—Know you ought of him?—Mercy, father!—mercy!

Sir Gilb. Listen, Rosalie—thy boy lives! (*She presses her father's hand, and watches his countenance, but is unable to articulate.*) Impressed with the idea—nay, convinced—that De Monneville was a villain, who had ruined and deserted you, I was driven to the verge of madness. You returned to London without proof of your marriage. I hastily visited France; I endeavoured to ease my tortured heart to discover the truth.

Ros. Fatality!

SIR GILB. I was in a wild and disordered state of mind; and, regardless of the horror it must have inflicted on your feelings, the boy was brought down privately to the country—if I condescended to look once at him, I own it was with the glance of a fiend.

Ros. Ah!

SIR GILB. I gave directions that the child should be removed from my sight—I even proceeded to the extremity to vow that I never would see him again. The statement of your friend Mordaunt, however, recalled my sympathy, an I lost not a moment in hastening to London to hold you again to my heart, and, Rosalie, to restore your lost son to you.

Ros. My unremitting prayers have been heard! Let me clasp my child in my fond embrace—we will never part again. (SIR GILBERT *goes off at the side.*) I hear his little footsteps? Dear, dear William! he comes! my head swims with joy—he comes.

(SIR GILBERT *leads on* DICK—*the boy abashed, and his face withdrawn—*ROSALIE *totters towards him—kneels, gazes wildly at him, pauses, and in a hurried manner passes her hand over the boy's forehead.*)

Ros. Merciful goodness!—no—what mockery is this?

SIR GILB. Rosalie!

Ros. (*Shuddering.*) This is not my child. Away! hence! Sear not a mother's heart. This last blow will deprive me of reason. Torture! pity! pity me!

(SIR GILBERT *approaches* ROSALIE—*she recoils from him, and faints in* LUCY'S *arms. Scene closes in on the group.*

E

SCENE III.

Room at MR. STRAWBERRY's.

Enter MR. STRAWBERRY, *with a Newspaper.* R. H.

STRAWB. Last night's debate—the ayes had it—to be sure—
(*Reads*)—" The concluding part of the Honorable Member's
speech was rendered perfectly inaudible by the cries of
hear ! hear ! from all sides of the House." Gad, how anxious
they must have been to listen to it ! I wonder what effect
my maiden effort will produce—(*Reads*)—" Roars of laugh-
ter :" that's an ominous coincidence.

Enter JACOB. L. H.

Well, Jacob, where is your mistress?

JACOB. Miss Prudence has gone out in a sedan chair, sir.

STRAWB. A sedan chair ! ha ! ha !

JACOB. Yes, sir, mistress be gone to call on the two Honorable Miss Starchblossoms at St. James's.

STRAWB. The Honorable Miss Starchblossoms ! Ah, I
remember they were the reigning toasts in about the middle
of George the Third's time.

JACOB. She told me to have the place tidy, as she were
going a shoplifting.

STRAWB. What !

JACOB. Shopping, I mean ; and as you said something
about toasts, they mayhap will all return here together to
take chocolate.

STRAWB. (*Apart.*) A nest of antiquated virgins ! who
would be so cruel as to go a bird's nesting.

JACOB. May I be so bold, as to remind you, sir, that you
are to hire a footboy ?

STRAWB. Ay, I recollect I am going down to the house this afternoon, and I'll see if any one wants a place. Where's the little black boy I sent to be white-washed?

JACOB. Oh, Mary, housemaid and the slopseller ha' made a nice little chap of him now, I sent him up into the drawing-room. (*Exit.*) L. H.

STRAWB. Hem! I long to see my rescued victim. (*Runs his eye over the newspaper.*) " Horrid brutality"—" Was married yesterday"—"Warranted quiet in harness"—" Should this meet the eye of the young gentleman who left his home, he is requested to"—" Use Rowland's Macassar Oil."— (*Exit.*) L. H.

SCENE IV.

The Drawing Room. Side-Window. An Arm Chair with practicable seat. Table with two vases of flowers, hand screen, &c. A bonnet.

The BOY *sings without, "* Cherry ripe! Cherry ripe!" &c. *and enters, neatly dressed, laughing.* R. H.

BOY. Ha! ha! (*admiring himself.*) I declare I don't know myself again; here's a nice jacket, and a clean collar. How happy I am! I can't make up my mind with the change, whether I ought to cry or to laugh. If I could but just peep at myself in the glass—now I feel as if I ought to cry. (*Sobs.—He gets on a chair before a mirror, bursts out laughing.*)—Oh, you dear little fellow—how glad I am to see you again! you pretty little fellow! (*Jumps down.*) Oh, I can't help singing for joy.

Enter STRAWBERRY.

STRAWB. Ah! ah! ah! this is something like; you are gentleman Billy, now.

BOY. Oh, sir, I am so happy, that I cannot help singing.

STRAWB. Sing away, then—there, there's half-a-crown for you.

BOY. My filth and rags removed—I have had such a breakfast—I assure you, sir, that I feel quite another man. (*Crosses to and fro.*)

STRAWB. What a change! I vow he has the air of a gentleman—how wonderful for a sweep (*looking at him*), and so handsome! my Climbing Boy is quite a chimney ornament.

BOY. If you please, sir, may I look out of the window?

STRAWB. Do what you like, child, but don't tumble into the street (*Goes up to chair, and sits*).

BOY. (*Goes to window and opens it.*) Oh, if the other poor boys could see me now! Aha! hurrah! hurrah! there he goes yonder—Hoy! holloa (*calls*) hoy!

STRAWB. Don't make such a noise, the people will think the house is on fire. What do you see?

BOY. (*Beckoning at the window.*) What do I see? Oh, sir, it is my friend, my best friend—I—I—mean the next best friend to you I have in the world.

STRAWB. You have a friend, then?

BOY. A true-hearted friend—he once gave my late master, Mr. Scroggins, a black eye for beating me.

STRAWB. Your friend must be a clever fellow to give a sweep a black eye.

BOY. When I was starving with cold and hunger, he brought me piping-hot roasted potatoes.

STRAWB. A philanthropist! I must know him. What is you friend's name?

BOY. Jack. Oh, sir, there isn't such a good fellow in all London.

STRAWB. Enumerate his good qualities.

Boy. If Jack sees a poor dog running mad, with a tin-kettle tied to his tail, he will stop him and release him from his misery—if any one beats his donkey, Jack sets his eye upon him and threatens him with Betty Martin. He won't allow cocks to fight in the street, but always parts them, and says,

> " Their little hands were never made
> To tear each others' eyes."

Strawb. Ha! ha! ha! I should like to be introduced to this paragon of humble virtue.

Boy. Please sir, may I go down stairs, sir, and ask Jack how he is? (*Apart*) I'll give him all the money I have got. Poor Jack! kind Jack!

Strawb. Go, bring him in. Let me speak to your friend.

Boy. Yes, sir, oh yes, sir. (*The boy runs across, and stops suddenly at the door.*) Yes, sir, I forgot myself, sir—sir!

(Strawberry *turns his head; the boy bows gravely, and exit.*) L. H.

Strawb. He certainly has a manner—this is an eventful day with me. What care I for being thought eccentric? Any thing to relieve my mind from that confounded maiden-speech—I wish I could procure a second-hand maiden speech, or an old maiden-speech, one that some other country member had left off, and was not much the worse for wear.

Boy. (*Without*). I tell you Jack, you are to come in.

Jack. (*Without*). Bless you I musn't—more than that, I dussn't.

Strawb. Eh, modest as well as virtuous! Bring your friend in, bring in the professor of humanity. (*The boy enters,* L. H. *pulling in* Jack *by the hand.*) Hang it! that's not a figure for a philanthropist.

Boy. Don't be shamefaced, Jack; the gentleman wont eat you, he has adopted me.

Jack. What's he done?

Boy (*To Jack*). Clothed me, fed me, and taken me entirely from my master.

Jack. Then one of my duties is over.

Boy. What, supplying me with victuals?

Jack. No, that was nothing. But I shan't have to whop old Mr. Scroggins any more, for not behaving like a gentleman to you.

Strawb. It appears that you have ever been kind to this little fellow?

Boy. Ay, that he has.

Jack. I'd a-done the same to any other little fellow when I seed him ill-used.

Strawb. I like that now. What is your name?

Jack. A rum 'un, sir. Jack Ragg, if you please, sir.

Strawb. Jack Ragg! Um!—have you been brought up to any business?

Jack. Oh yes, sir.

Strawb. What profession?

Jack. Crossing-sweeping (*shows stump of a broom*)—Ah! trade is very bad now—there's a general stagnation in our business.

Strawb. Ha! ha! ha! go on Mr. Ragg, ha! ha!

Jack. (*Aside.*) Mr. Ragg, he is laughing at me.

Strawb. Well!

Jack. I shouldn't have done that.

Strawb. What, I say?

Jack. I shouldn't ha' done that.

Strawb. What?

Jack. That. Never ridicule the poor.

STRAWB. (*Apart.*) Egad, this fellow has sentiment about him. There, Jack Ragg, put your pleasant looks on again ; my little boy here can tell you whether or not I can be kind.

JACK. Gentleman Billy was a sweep once—I am now ; we were in different lines to be sure—he, chimbleys ! I, crossings ! he was in the narrow way, sir, and I was in the broad-way : but the bad debts runs away with all the profits of my business. I dare say I'm owed a matter of a hundred pounds.

STRAWB. Indeed ! a large sum for one in your situation.

JACK. My situation was a good 'un—from the corner of the Haymarket to Cockspur-street.

STRAWB. Well, but a hundred pounds ! how can you make that appear ?

JACK. Ecod, I wish I could make it appear. But d'ye see, sir, gentlefolks walks over my clean crossing without dirtying their boots. " Pray remember the poor sweeper !" says I. " I'll give you something as I come back, boy," says they ; catch them coming back again. Bless you, the credit I have given to people of the first fashion is unknown ; now I shouldn't have done that, should I, Billy ?

BOY. No, no ! Jack, you are too honest.

STRAWB. But, my poor fellow, have you no other mode of getting your bread ?

JACK. Yes, when one branch of commerce fails, I tries another. I have stood at a pump all day, and pumped for every body. Sometimes a servant-maid will give me a penny, the stingy ones offer me a drink of water out of the mug for my trouble, as if I hadn't got a mug of my own. So I puts one mug on the top of the other. (*Shows his hat with the crown knocked in.*)

STRAWB. Ha ! ha ! the water-works did not answer ?

JACK. It did for the day. At night I commenced another commercial concern, sold penny play-bills at the theatre door. House bill! Theatrical Observer! Correct bill of the performance!—But that business, I am sorry to say, has declined too—Ah! it's no joke—nothing moving now but stagnation—stagnation.

STRAW. (*Apart.*) I recollect—I am to hire a foot-boy—(*To* JACK.) Can you brush boots?

JACK. Why I brush my own, sir. (*Looks at his broom.*)

STRAWB. If I were inclined to try you as an errand-boy, who would give you a character?

BOY. I will.

STRAWB. *You?* ha! ha! what do you know about his last place?

JACK. My last place was a post.

STRAWB. A post?

JACK. And I can have a three years' character from it. But, however, I've shut up shop for to-day.

STRAWB. Shut up shop—why how d'ye mean? I thought you worked in the open air, ha! ha! ha!

JACK. What we call shutting up shop—before we goes away, we sweeps the mud all over the crossin' again—that's shutting up shop.—

STRAWB. I like the humour of the fellow, and I will endeavour to reclaim this well-intentioned lad from the streets. (*To* JACK) Stay you here a moment; I must consult Jacob. (*Calls*) Jacob!

JACOB. (*Without.*) Sir, I be getting mistress' chocolate ready again she comes home.

STRAWB. Oh! I'll come to you then. (*Exit.*) L. H.

JACK. Gentleman Billy, boy—here's a circumbendibus.

Boy. Mr. Strawberry says he'll take you for a servant. Now, don't you go, and be too proud and refuse.

JACK. Only let him ax me—there are three capital reasons which I feel internally for taking a footman's place, and those are—breakfast, dinner and supper; but I say, Billy—Gentleman Billy I mean, we shall have no more first of May business, you know. Did you tell that respectable old buffer that I was ever my Lady Poll with the Jack-in-the-green?

Boy. Oh, no!

JACK. Then, perhaps, you'd as well not—he mayn't be so fond of dancing as you and I were?

Boy. Ah, Jack, if it were only for the holiday from hard labour, that first of May used to make us so merry.

JACK. Don't forget the roast beef and plumb-pudding.—But good-bye to the first of May, we shall never have your cheeks and legs touched up with rose-pink again.

Boy. No more gilt jackets, flowers, and feathers—ha! ha!

JACK. With our Chancellor of the Chequers with his salt-box, with a slit in the top for the ha'pence—heigho!—Eh, do you remember Bob smugging them out of the bottom —the nasty beast?

DUET.—(*Parody*.)

AIR.—" As it fell upon a day.—(*Bishop*.)

Boy *and* JACK.

Oh! dear, what a joyous day
Was the merry first of May;
Leaving off your sooty bags,
Dress'd in party-coloured rags,
Sweeps did skip,
While drums did roll,
So lighty trips
My lady Poll.

JACK. Billy, let's have a regular first of May dance;
it's the last.—There's nobody by but you and I.

> (*The Band plays a lively air.* BOY *takes up a hand-
> screen and a round ruler from the Table, and trips
> round in the customary fashion.* JACK *puts on a bon-
> net hind part before; takes out seat of a large arm-
> chair, gets between the legs, and holding it up by the
> arms, substitutes it for the Jack-in-the-Green. They
> are dancing joyously.*)

BOY. (*Bawls*) Only once a year, my lady.

> (*Enter* MISS STRAWBERRY, *and the* MISSES STARCH-
> BLOSSOM; *they stand in mute astonishment.* JACOB
> *enters with Chocolate Cups on waiter, which is over-
> turned by* JACK'S *Chair in swinging round. Ladies
> shriek. Enter* STRAWBERRY; *he is amazed, confused.*
> JACK *and* BOY *in despair.*)

END OF ACT II.

ACT III.—SCENE I.

Entrance Hall in MR. STRAWBERRY's *London House. A Fire-place. Sedan Chair. Street Door.*

Enter MISS STRAWBERRY, *followed by* JACOB. R. H.

MISS STRAWB. What?—Do you mean to say, Jacob, that whilst I was out, my brother has hired that ragged ruffian that was dancing in the arm-chair, as a footboy!

JACOB. It be his humanity, you know, ma'am.

MISS STRAWB. Humanity—ridiculous! insanity!—Mr. Strawberry's humanity is of that nature; he would bring in a bill in the House for erecting an infirmary for mad bulls!—

JACOB. Bless his heart, ma'am, ay!—he is so kind and tender, that he would take the trouble to hold an umbrella over a duck in a shower of rain! I've seen him do it.

MISS STRAWB. I am wearied out with his freaks—And, pray, when is this wretch to come into the house as servant?

JACOB. To-day, ma'am; master has sent him wi' a note to a clothes emporium—as the card says—to get him fitted out as footboy.—(*A long and loud knock at the street-door.*)

MISS STRAWB. A carriage knock—Bless my soul! company—don't open the door, Jacob, till I am seated and arranged in the parlour—and, d'ye hear? when your master comes in, ask him for my Tompion.

JACOB. Your Tom—what, ma'am?

MISS STRAWB. My Tompion watch, I lent him last night to hang at his bed's-head. (*Exit* MISS STRAWBERRY.)

JACOB. Oh—ah—Now for the door.—(*As he approaches it, another loud knock,* JACOB *opens it respectfully.*)

Enter JACK RAGG, *in a livery that does not fit him ; he struts into the hall.*

JACOB. (*Astonished.*) And is that you ?—alone !—

JACK. Yes—What do you think of me ?

JACOB. What do I think—I think you are an impudent rascal, coming with such a knock as that.

JACK. How am I ever to get my hand in, if I don't practise ?

JACOB. I never heard anything like it !

JACK. But I have—I heard a footman give just such another rat-tat-tat-tat-tat-tat-tat, with a carriage, at a door in the next street—I say, old 'un, where's gentleman Billy ?

JACOB. This will never do. (*Takes* JACK's *hat off.*)

JACK. What ?—O—ay hang it up somewhere—there's a good boy.

JACOB. Your disrespectful manners !—I am afraid master has made a great mistake in hiring you.

JACK. No he hasn't—see how I'll work when I begin.

JACOB. Well, then, begin.

JACK. Where's the table-beer ?—What shall I begin upon ?

JACOB. (*Aside.*) I'll frighten him with too much to do. Go down stairs and ask the cook for all the dirty knives and forks, rub them on the board—fill the coal skuttles—

JACK. With the knives and forks ?

JACOB. No, fool ;—then clean the candlesticks, empty the snuffers, fetch pump-water, wash down the area, brush out the cistern, black all the boots and shoes you can find, crocus-powder the tea-urn, leather the glasses—

JACK. None of your gammon, old cock. Leather the glasses—Oh, ha ! ha !—leather the glasses—sha'n't I break some of them ?

JACOB. Psha !—idiot—Rinse the decanters, dust the china, rub the mahogany tables, clean the windows, trim the lamps, wind up the jack and the kitchen clock, put every thing in its place, and then brush my great coat, till you are ordered to do something else.

JACK. Is that all ?

JACOB. Yes, take and do it, (*aside*) while I devise a scheme to get rid of you and the other rip from the streets. (*Exit* JACOB.) R. H.

JACK. There's a crusty old buffer.—(*Looks round.*)— What is this black thing in the corner here, like Punch's puppet-show in mourning ?—Oh, ay—that is a sedan-chair—queer sort of carriage, patronized by the elderly ladies, because they love to be supported by *two* of the male creation—it's a conceited-looking concern. A one-horse chay for my money—(when I have any)—ha ! ha !— I never see a one-horse chay without thinking of the adventure of Mr. and Mrs. Bubb at Brighton in their one-horse chay. I heard that at the Golden-Cross—ha ! ha !—

SONG.

TUNE—*" Eveleen's Bower."* (*The words selected.)*

Mrs. Bubb was gay and free, fair, fat, and forty-three—
  And blooming as a peony in buxom May ;
The toast she long had been of Farringdon Within,
  And she filled the better half of a one-horse chay.

Mrs. Bubb said to her lord, " You can well, Bubb, afford
  Whate'er a Common-council-man in prudence may,—
We've no brats to plague our lives, and the soap concern it thrives,
  Let's have a trip to Brighton in our one-horse chay.

" We'll view the pier and shipping, and enjoy many a dipping,
  And walk for an appetite in smart array ;
I longs more than I can utter, for shrimps and bread and butter,
  And an airing on the Steyne in the one-horse chay."

F

When at Brighton they were housed, and had stuff'd and carous'd,
  O'er a bowl of rack punch, Mr. Bubb did say,—
" I've ascertained, my dear, the mode of bathing here,
  From the ostler who is cleaning up my one-horse chay.

" Our old horse for sartin, may be trusted gig or cart in,
  And shillings for machines I sha'nt throw away ;
He'll stand like any post, while we dabble on the coast,
  And get in sly to dress in our one-horse chay."

So out they drove all drest, so gaily in their best,
  And finding in their rambles a snug little bay,
They uncased at their leisure, paddled out to take the pleasure,
  And left their clothes behind in the one-horse chay.

But while so snugly sure that all things were secure,
  They flounced about like porpoises or whales at play,
Some young unlucky imps, who prowl'd about for shrimps,
  Soon gudgeon'd the contents of the one-horse-chay.

When our pair were soused enough, and returned in their buff,
  Oh, there was the vengeance of old Nick to pay ;
Madam shriek'd in consternation, Mr. Bubb he swore " damnation !"
  To find the empty state of his one-horse chay.

" Come bundle in with me, we must squeeze for once," says he,
  " And manage this here business the best we may ;"
So, as dismal as two dummies, their heads stuck out like mummies
  From beneath the little apron of the one-horse chay.

The Steyne was in a throng, as they jogg'd it along,
  Madam had'nt been so put to it for many a day,—
O ! the trouble and the rout, to wrap and get them out,
  When they drove to their lodgings in the one-horse chay.

Ha ! ha ! With my one-horse chay, I forgot the sedan chair.
La ! I've seen the gentlewomen and countesses going to
court in them, bobbing up and down with their ear-rings
resting on their hips. I wonder what is inside—I should

like to look. The door is in the front, and, ah! it opens, some how so, at the top, like a salt-box. Dear me!—(*Goes in.*)—Ha! ha! here's a queer little shop! What a carriage! licensed to carry one inside.

JACOB. (*Without.*) John!—John Ragg!

JACK (*having shut himself in the sedan, cannot get out—looks from the side window.*) I say, though, I can't get out—curstnation! I'm cotch'd like a rat in a trap. The door won't open, and I'm too fat to get out o' the window. He comes! I feel like a rat now; I hope he won't bring the old cat with him. I'll sit quite still—I'll be as quiet as the Charleys used to be in their watch-boxes.—" Past three." What a nice little place this would be to stand up in, in a shower of rain—(*Rises, knocks his head*)—Can't stand up, though.—(*Reclines in sedan chair.*)

Enter JACOB.—(*He looks about.*)

JACOB. What has become of that scamp, Jack Ragg? I won't live in an honest service with such a mangy hound. I've hit on a plan to settle his business, and make Mr. Strawberry turn both sweepers into the street.

JACK. (*Apart.*) Eh!

JACOB. Didn't I hear a noise? Where has that fellow hid himself?—(*Looks off cautiously, at the sides.*)—Got outside the door again,—I am safe from observation.—(*Takes out an old-fashioned watch.*)—Here be Missis's Tompion—her Tompion watch. She lent it to master; he left it at his bed's-head. Here be the nasty little climbing boy's cap.—(*Shews it.*)—The watch discovered concealed in it, put in a convenient place, would thoroughly undermine both their characters: yonder stove,—a natural situation. Yes, there they shall go.

JACK. (*Observing.*) O, ho!—(*Aside.*)

JACOB. (*Going to the stove.*) I'll order Jenny to light the hall fire.

JACK. (*Aside.*) Oh!

JACOB. What was that?—(*Looks towards door.*)—Some one in the street.—(*Crossing.*) The chimney will smoke, the cause will be inquired—the spoil, and, ha!—it will be *a spoil*—must be discovered. Jenny! Jenny, I say! (*Exit* JACOB.) R. H.

JACK. (*Looking out of the sedan.*) Light the hall fire—you will have a fire lighted under you. But how am I to get out?—(*Tries the door of the sedan, and struggles again at the window.*)

Re-enter JACOB, *with his hat.*

JACK. (*Hiding himself in the sedan.*) Somebody else!

JACOB. I have given the girl her directions; and now, having accomplished this matter to my satisfaction, I'll go and witness the foundation of pious Mr. Mackcorkmyjoy's new chapel. (*Opens street door, and exit.*) C. D.

JACK. You are a precious fellow to go to chapel. Well, but, thunder and tripe! how am I to get out of this black leather watch-box. Somebody else!

Enter the MAID, *with articles to light the fire.*

JACK. Done again—they must not find me here. Is she going to chapel?—(*As the girl is preparing to light the fire, a knock at the door.—Mr.* CHIFFONIER *enters.*)

JACK. (*Apart.*) Somebody else!

MAID. (*Opening door.*) Your business, sir? Oh, Mr. Chiffonier, who let the house to us.

CHIFF. Yes, my dear; I am come for the picture—the portrait of the lady in the green bed-chamber. I have Madame De Monneville's directions to take it to her. (*Exit.*) R. H.

MAID (*Attempts to light the fire.*)—Very odd: what is the matter with the stove, there is no draught in it?

Enter from the room door MISS STRAWBERRY.

JACK. (*Apart.*) Somebody else!

MAID. Please, ma'am, I can't get this fire to light.

JACK. (*Looks out.*) Oh, murder! there's old pussy.— (*Hides himself.*)

MISS STRAWB. Perhaps, Jenny, the stove is damp. How strange, that my Tompion watch has not been returned to me! London is a vile place; I hope the watch has not been stolen. Jenny, did you look in my brother's bed-room for it?

MAID. Yes, 'um: and it warn't there.

MISS STRAWB. I suspect that little sweep of having purloined it.

Re-enter CHIFFONIER, *with the picture.* R. H.

Hey-day! what is all this?

JACK. (*Apart.*) Somebody else!

CHIFF. The picture belongs to the proprietress of this mansion—I have her orders to remove it. Madam, you don't know me; I am Mr. Chiffonier, the upholsterer;—I let Mr. Strawberry the house. You are almost as peremptory as the little lad I found in the bed-room up stairs, gazing on this picture; he was crying his eyes out, because we removed it, poor child. (*Exit.*) C. D.

Enter the BOY, *running.* R. H.

JACK. (*Apart.*) Somebody else!

MISS STRAWB. Pray, have you seen a watch of mine, sirrah?

BOY. No, madam. Yes—yes, I will not lose sight of it— I'll run after them.—(*Apart*) It is my mother. (*Exit, at the hall-door, unperceived.*)

Maid. (*Suddenly*) Ma'am, please ma'am, I've found something in the flue—all black (*produces the sweep's cap.*) And here inside—eh, what is it?

Jack. (*Apart*) Somebody else!

Maid. La, ma'am, here's your watch!

Miss Strawb. My Tompion, as I live! concealed there in the sweep's cap. Ah! I thought as much. You little villain. Oh, you young rascal—where is he—ah! decamped—now—now, I shall have my triumph over my silly brother. The depredator is vanished, though my watch is safe. I wonder where the other wretch is?

Jack. (*Apart*) Somebody else!

Miss Strawb. Quick, Jenny, open the door, and call in the police—you are a witness to the whole of it.

Maid. Yes, ma'am. (*Exit at door.*)

Miss Strawb. This will be a pretty lesson to my brother, harbouring rogues and vagabonds out of the streets—it is lucky we are not all murdered in our beds.—(Jack Ragg *sneezes, very loudly, in the sedan.*) Bless, my soul! what was that? the noise was in the house. The servants are all out. (Jack *sneezes again.*) It is in the sedan-chair—how I palpitate—horrible—there is a man in that sedan (*goes to the street door.*) Oh! I shall faint—help—help—help!

(Jack Ragg *makes a ludicrous struggle to get out at the window of the chair.*)

Jack. I am too fat. I wish I was a live eel.

Miss Strawb. Ugh! the wretch will annihilate me.—Jenny, Jenny! help—help—help!

Re-enter Jenny, *with two Policemen.*

Jack. Somebody else!

Miss Strawb. Oh, gentlemen, I'm so happy you are

come—there has been a robbery committed in the house; and a confederate of the thief is at this moment hid in that sedan chair;—seize him!

(*The Police men go up to the chair;* JACK *looks out at top.*)

JACK. Hear me—it's all gammon. I am hired as footman here to Mr. Raspberry. I'm as honest as a babe unborn.— Where's gentleman Billy? send for gentleman Billy.—I'm Mr. Gooseberry's footboy, I tell you—where's Billy?

MISS STRAWB. He speaks of his companion, who attempted to steal this watch—don't let him out, the wretch will do me an injury; he is wild, violent—mad—he danced about in an arm-chair with the bottom out.

1st POL. Egad, we had better take him to the station as he is in the sedan, he is locked in safe.

MISS STRAWB. Any how, so as you convey him away— but bring back the sedan, as it is hired.

(*The Policemen lift up the chair, and are making their way out of the street door;* JACK *tries to address them, first from one window, and then from the other, bearing the chair down on each side.*)

JACK. I appeal to your sensi*bilittities* (*looks out at the other window.*) I'm an Englishman (*goes to the opposite side.*) I speak to you as gentlemen (*turns to the opposite window.*) D'ye call this the constitution?

(*The Policemen carry the sedan out at the hall door.* MISS STRAWBERRY *and* JENNY *exeunt, exclaiming—* " Carry him away.")

SCENE II.

An Apartment in Sir Gilbert Thorncliffe's *House in London.*

Enter Rebecca *and* Dick.   r. h.

Reb. La! deary me, Dick, I'm tired of this large town; I shall ax Sir Gilbert's leave to let us go back again to the Park Lodge—put on your hat, boy.—You remember the way we walked to Muster Strawberry's house in the square? —go, ring the bell, and see your father—tell him he must get permission to come here directly—then run you back again—scamper. (Dick *runs off.* r. h.)   That teasing old Jacob Buzzard—now isn't it a shame that so nice a young 'oman as I am, should be neglected, like a decayed flower; but I'll tell you a bit o' my mind, mister husband, if you can't contrive to give me a little more of your company, I knows them as will.

Mr. Strawb. (*Without.*) Is Sir Gilbert Thorncliffe within? No.   I must wait for him then. (*Enters.* r. h.) Here's a trouble and a fuss.   Oh, why the devil was I ever born with the organ of humanity on some part of my head—all my warm-hearted feeling thrown away, all my kindness crushed?   The naughty boy—to steal my sister's Tompion, Oh, that wretched—wretched boy!

Reb. (*Apart.*) What does he say about a boy?

Strawb. To come into my house, and just now, when my back was turned, to commit a robbery—and the child had such an innocent look.

Reb. (*Apart.*) Innocent look?   Sure, he don't mean my Dick.

Strawb. "But fast bind, safe find," as poor Richard says.

REB. (*Apart.*) *Poor Richard*—it must be poor Dick.

STRAWB. I shall begin and suspect Jacob Buzzard next.

REB. Oh—mercy!

STRAWB. I—I would have spared the poor boy; but my sister has sent the police after him. Ah—(*sees* REBECCA)—bless my soul, little Rebecca—are you in London? This is an unexpected pleasure.

REB. Thank ye, sir—hope madam is well—you were speaking of a little boy, sir.

STRAWB. Yes, a young rascal, though I'm sorry to say it to you, whom I have been kind to, not half a quarter of an hour ago, stole my sister's watch. Ah! Rebecca, with all my merciful feelings, I should be sorry to be that boy's mother.

REB. Sir, I am sure you must be mistaken—I certainly sent the boy there—you have been good to the child, and I am sure he would not make so ungrateful a return. Oh—oh—oh! pity him—pity him! (*Sobs, and becomes hysterical.*)

STRAWB. Poor creature, how she's affected?—what puts you in such a way? She will faint. Help—help! I say!—(*Catches* REBECCA *in his arms.*) Rebecca, I say.—Lauk! how pretty she looks, although she has fainted.—Rebecca, you little rogue—come to. (*Kisses her cheek, slyly*).

Enter JACOB BUZZARD, *suddenly.* R. H.

JACOB. (*As he enters*) I ha' seen the foundation laid.—Eh—what, master, the honeysuckle window!—Sir—sir—(STRAWBERRY *runs off.*—JACOB *walks up and down distractedly.*)

REB. Jacob! Jacob! You don't know what has happened to me?

JACOB. I think *I do*—though.

Reb. I have every fear—I, I sent Dick to you, to—

Jacob. To get him out of the way, I suppose.

Reb. No, no! on my soul, Jacob—Ah! your cruel suspicions—but Dick has not returned—and—from what I could gather from Mr. Strawberry just now—which put me in such a flurry—the boy is taken up for stealing Miss Strawberry's watch.

Jacob (*starts*). Eh—how?

Enter a Policeman. r. h.

Police. Is your name Rebecca Buzzard? if so, you must come with me to the station—a robbery has been committed by a boy at a house in the square—a child, who says he is your son, was observed loitering about the premises, and he is in custody—there is no present proof against him, but we must detain him.

Reb. I will attend you instantly—follow, Jacob—follow. I am sure my dear boy is innocent.

[*Exeunt* Rebecca *and the* Policeman. r. h.

Jacob (*thoughtfully*). Caught in my own trap; what's to be done? I must see how the land lies clearly before I confess. (*Exit.*) r. h.

SCENE III.

Another Room in the Mansion of Sir Gilbert Thorncliffe. *Portrait discovered against Table. Music on the Table, &c.*

(*The* Boy *enters.*) r. h. 2 e.

Boy. So I've made my way into the house where they have brought the picture—this has been an eventful day for me—some one comes. (*He hides behind the table.*)

Enter Sir Gilbert Thorncliffe. L. H.

Sir Gilb. Tell my daughter I request to see her. Ah! that portrait! how it recalls a thousand fond feelings—endearments I enjoyed before my heart was seared! Poor Rosalie! where, ah! where, now is the poor boy whom I abandoned—discarded? My grandson, should he be in existence, will inherit my large estate.

Enter Rosalie. L. H.

Dearest Rosalie—

Ros. Welcome! father. Welcome!

Sir Gilb. I have accounted, my love, for the painful error I committed, as regarded the child I introduced to you.

Ros. Spare me!

Sir Gilb. I am not surprised at that shudder, my daughter; the villain who wickedly imposed on me shall be severely punished—but, Rosalie, come, cheer thee, my love; it is long since I have heard the touching tones of your voice; and—(*goes to table*) ah! here is an old favourite melody. Rosalie, my daughter—endeavour to recall former times to me.

Ros. (*Kissing his hand.*) Father! this—this does recall former times. I will attempt a ballad I taught my poor lost boy to sing.

SONG.—*French Air.* (*The words selected.*)

Beneath a lattice, ivy-wove,
  A Troubadour is singing;
He calls unto his lady-love,
  " Thy chamber prithee, sweet, forsake!
" Nor longer tarry there!
  " Haste away! haste away!
" The sun's last kiss has press'd the lake,
  " A kindred rapture flinging,
" And the blushes bright appear,
  " Rushing as in fear—
" Down its bosom late so clear.

" Then haste away—
" No more delay—
" Lest the envious darkness veils the blush,
" More lovely far than the lake's deep flush—
" Then hast away—love—
" Haste away !—away !—"

Beside that water's moonlight gleam,
   His lady-love is sighing –
The misty wreaths of morning's beam
   Remind her of Time's rapid flight.
" Farewell !" she cries, " Farewell !
   " Fare thee well ! Fare thee well !—
" I've watched the thickly growing night—
   " The gorgeous sun hue dying—
" And what seem'd like gold to be,
" As if by alchemy
" Transmuted, now is silvery.
      " Then haste away,
      " Ere break of day
" Throws distant shadows o'er the lake—"
They pause—they kiss—the last they take—
      Then sigh, " Farewell !
      " Fare thee well—love—
      " Fare thee well !—away !—"

(SIR GILBERT *presses* ROSALIE'S *hand affectionately. The*
   BOY *sings the last line, behind the picture*—" Fare thee
   well !—away.")

Ros. Merciful goodness ! the voice of my child !

(*The* BOY *runs forward and kneels before* ROSALIE, *uttering*
   " Dear Mother ! Mother !")

Ros. My love, my William—Ah ! the happiness in again
embracing you, and pressing your little hand—my adored
boy.

Boy. Sweet mother, these kisses repay my sufferings. I should have died but for one friend—Mother, dear mother, you must be good to Jack—I'm sure you will be kind to Jack.

Ros. Again restored to me, after four years of unremitting wretchedness!—no wish of yours shall be refused. Sir Gilbert—father, permit me for a few minutes to retire with my long-lost child—and to offer up my fervent prayers for the blessing of his restoration to me.

[*Exeunt* ROSALIE *and* BOY. L. H.

Enter MR. STRAWBERRY. R. H.

STRAWB. Oh! Sir Gilbert—ever since I have resided in London—one day only—I've been like the ladies gowns and caps, all puckers—and, ah! my worthy colleague, my greatest pucker is to come.

SIR GILB. And what may that be, sir?

STRAWB. My maiden-speech.

SIR GILB. Mr. Strawberry, I was about to write to you—as it is, I regret exceedingly to be the bearer of disagreeable intelligence—but—

STRAWB. Ah! I know—I shall go down to the House to-night, and make a great gaby of myself—I am perfectly aware of that.

SIR GILB. Pardon me,—hurried away by their zeal, your agents at the election were incautious—

STRAWB. Yes! they contrived to return me member—and I am to commit myself in a speech—a mad maiden-speech—

SIR GILB. I fear, sir—that you will be relieved from the necessity of doing so.

STRAWB. You don't say it? (*Joyfully.*) I'd chop off my right-arm to be quit of it.

G

Sɪʀ Gɪʟʙ. It is a painful necessity—I am under the apprehension, that from the state of the case before the committee, and I say it with the deepest feelings of regret that——

Sᴛʀᴀᴡʙ. What!—go on—go on—relieve me from suspense.

Sɪʀ Gɪʟʙ. That your seat in the honourable House is lost entirely. You are no longer a member of parliament.

Sᴛʀᴀᴡʙ. Are you sure you are correct?

Sɪʀ Gɪʟʙ. Painfully I repeat it—positively!

Sᴛʀᴀᴡʙ. Ahem! (*Sings.*) "Nancy Dawson was a——" beg pardon, Sir Gilbert, "tol de rol, de rol—ti tum, ti tum, ti ti tum,"——and I really am ejected:—ha! ha! ha!—Shake hands, Sir Gilbert?

Sɪʀ Gɪʟʙ. Extraordinary! Why, what do you mean, Mr. Strawberry?

Sᴛʀᴀᴡʙ. Mean! Why, that I have attained the height of human happiness, in being turned out.—Look'ye, Sir Gilbert, I never sought it—and I never bought it—and plague take those who buy that which common honesty forbids to be sold. I have nothing to do with a party—unless I invite a jolly party to dinner—I give you my honour, sir, that I am relieved from a great load of anxiety, by being ousted.

Sɪʀ Gɪʟʙ. Astonishing!

Sᴛʀᴀᴡʙ. Not a bit; think of the maiden-speech I had to make at sixty years of age—I said just now, that I would rather have lost an arm than have attempted it; but here, ha! ha!—huzza! instead of losing an arm, I only lose my seat. Ha! ha! ha!

(*Voices without*—Pᴏʟɪᴄᴇ Iɴsᴘᴇᴄᴛᴏʀ. The boy must go with me.—Lᴜᴄʏ. Sir Gilbert—where is Sir Gilbert?)

Sɪʀ Gɪʟʙ. Whence this confusion?

Enter Lucy, *hastily.* R. H.

Lucy. Oh! Sir Gilbert.

Sir Gilb. What is the matter?

Lucy. Oh, my poor mistress!

Sir Gilb. What of your mistress?

Lucy. Sir—there was a knock the moment the door was opened, a police inspector entered, and said he had traced a boy here who had stolen a watch, he insisted on searching the house.

Strawb. It's all true, I fear, Sir Gilbert; an ungrateful young dog did steal my sister's watch—

Sir Gilb. Your's, sir—and that boy—surely there must be some mistake.

Lucy. Oh! pray, gentlemen, come down; my mistress is breaking her heart about it. (*To* Mr. Strawberry) Your sister is below, sir.

Sir Gilb. We will follow you.   (*Exeunt.*) R. H.

SCENE LAST.

Parlour in Sir Gilbert's *house.* Rosalie *is discovered seated, clasping her son round the neck and weeping. The Police Inspector in attendance.* Miss Strawberry *in bonnet and cloak.*

Miss Strawb. Ah! my dear madam, it is useless weeping—the naughty child took my watch sure enough. I have never been a mother myself; but I can guess what your feelings must be in finding your son a thief——

Boy. A thief!—a thief!—ah! (*Hides his face in his hands.*) I am innocent—dear mother—innocent!

(*Enter* Lucy, Sir Gilbert *and* Strawberry.) R. H.

Sir Gilb. I am a magistrate, sir, (*to the* Inspector,)

and am competent to investigate this affair. Let Jacob—Mr. Strawberry's servant, be brought in. (*The* POLICEMAN *goes off.* L. H.)

MISS STRAWB. Ah! Jacob will set matters all as they should be, good old man.

STRAWB. Hold your tongue, sister.

MISS STRAWB. See the trouble, brother, that your non-sensical humanity has brought upon us all!

Enter JACOB, *his looks haggard and care-worn.* L.H.

SIR GILB. (*Sternly.*) Do you accuse this boy of the robbery?

JACOB. I accuse no one; it is not in my conscience to do it.

STRAWB. Ahem! (*Aside.*) His conscience lugged in again!

SIR GILB. What, then, do you know of the matter?

JACOB. How should I know any thing of it, sir? I was from home; I had my mistress's permission to go to see the first stone of the new chapel laid.

SIR GILB. Prior to your leaving the house, did you see the watch?

JACOB. Yes—eh?—yes, I saw it hanging at master's bed-head.

SIR GILB. And that is all you know of the matter?

JACOB. All—all.

MISS STRAWB. It is now my turn to say, that after I had given Jacob leave to witness the ceremony at Mr. M'Cork-myjoy's new chapel—I was in the hall—our maid, in lighting the fire, discovered my watch concealed in the Climbing Boy's cap in the stove. On my remonstrating with yonder little rogue (*pointing to the boy*) he rushed out at the street door, leaving his confederate, who is now in custody, hid in the sedan-chair which stood in the hall.

JACOB. (*Starts and trembles.*) The sedan chair !

SIR GILB. (*Aside, whispers to the* POLICE INSPECTOR.)

POLICE. He is below, sir ; I brought him here to recognize the boy. (*Goes off.*)

MISS STRAWB. It appeared that the odious wretch had been concealed there for a long time—for what purpose, I cannot possibly imagine. (*To* STRAWBERRY) This, brother, was another of your fine speculations ; but you would have had your house robbed, and your whole family murdered and flung in a ditch, sooner than relinquish your ridiculous hobbies.

STRAWB. (*Aside.*) A maiden-speech !—As I am no longer in Parliament, I shall not reply to it.

MISS STRAWB. What did you say ?

STRAWB. The honourable member uttered a few words that were inaudible.

JACK. (*Without.*) After you, sir, is manners.

Enter the POLICE INSPECTOR *and* JACK RAGG, REBECCA *and* DICK.

BOY. Ah ! there's Jack ! I'm so glad you've found him again.

JACK. I've been quite safe, gentleman William—the first time I was ever locked up. The moment I endeavoured to become respectable, and procure a place, I'm carried off to the police station.

SIR GILB. Pray, what business had you in the sedan ?

JACK. My lord, I can't say that I had either business or pleasure there. I got in, like a great fool, and couldn't get out again, and I was afraid of the anger of this here good lady.

SIR GILB. Then you were witness to the discovery of the Climbing Boy's cap in the stove ?

JACK. Yes—and I was witness, too, how it came there.

SIR GILB. Did that young boy put it in the chimney ?

JACK. No—but that *old* boy did (*pointing to* JACOB), and I wondered what the devil he could do it for.

OMNES. Jacob !—Impossible !

JACOB. Fie, fie—a sinful—a wicked invention !

JACK. It's no invention, but the naked truth, you *rampacious* old *willin ;* I saw you hide the watch in the boy's cap—I heard you call the maid to light the fire, that it might be discovered, to ruin poor gentleman Billy's character. I've a great mind to larrup you ; and if it warn't for the *P. in blue* there, I would. Ladies and gentlemen, if you don't believe what I say, let Jacob's coat-pocket be *sarched*—*sarch* him ! In handling the sweep's cap, he blacked his fingers—he wiped the soot off with his handkerchief. (*The* POLICE INSPECTOR *produces a handkerchief from* JACOB's *pocket, soiled with soot.*) Ah, ha ! old Belzeebub, are you *cotched* out at last ?

(SIR GILBERT *motions that* JACOB *should withdraw ;* REBECCA *places his. arm within hers ;* JACOB *looks round suspiciously at* MR. STRAWBERRY. *Exeunt* JACOB, REBECCA, DICK, *and the* POLICE.)

STRAWB. Well, egad ! it has all come right at last—eh, sister ?

MISS STRAWB. (*Confused.*) Brother, (*taking letters from her reticule*), here are some letters I want you to frank. I know you have the power to send eight, free of postage.

STRAWB. Ah ! where are they directed ?

MISS STRAWB. To our seat.

STRAWB. Burn your letters ! I go down to our seat in the country to-morrow, having happily got rid of my seat in town to-day.

MISS STRAWB. What! are you no longer a member?

STRAWB. Devil a bit. I am a country member—returned —no—no—henceforward I'll have nothing to do with the reins of government.

JACK RAGG. I've had something to do with the reins of government before now—beg pardon—

STRAWB. You? hear! hear! hear! what d'ye mean? what have you had to do with the reins of government?

JACK RAGG. 'Mongst other trades to earn an honest penny, I have often held the bridles of the horses of the Parliament men, while they were up stairs settling the nation in the house of Doctors' Commons.

STRAWB. Ha! ha! ha! Well, we have had an out-of-the-way wild plot and incidents with our little history of *The Climbing Boy*. The humanity of our friends will forgive the eccentricity, and although we shall not send the little fellow up the chimney again, may we be permitted to retain him in his present happy condition, assured of *-- smiles and approbation?

FINALE.

All kind souls this hour befriend us,
Cheer the Climbing Boy's sad heart;
Sympathy we prithee lend us,
And disarm the critic's dart.

Ros. See a mother now is pleading
With the eloquence of tears,
Tears of joy, at length regaining
The object of her hopes and fears.

Chorus.

All kind souls, &c.

JACK.   Billy, dear, you've changed your suit, man,
                   Soot no longer stains your face.

MISS STRAWB. Silence, you are only footman.

JACK.   Thank you, ma'am, I'll keep my place.

Chorus.

All kind souls, &c.

THE END.

BAYLIS AND LEIGHTON,
JOHNSONS'-COURT, FLEET-STREET.

CPSIA information can be obtained at www.ICGtesting.com
Printed in the USA
BVOW04s1110180914

367402BV00025B/499/P